POCKET GUIDE TO
Knitting

Take-Along Information on Tools, Basics, Tips, and Tricks

Jen Lucas

T0357008

Landauer Publishing

POCKET GUIDE TO KNITTING

Landauer Publishing, www.landauerpub.com, is an imprint of Fox Chapel Publishing Company, Inc.

Project Team
Managing Editor: Gretchen Bacon
Acquisitions Editor: Amelia Johanson
Editor: Christa Oestreich
Designer: Freire Disseny + Comunicació

ISBN 978-1-63981-073-4

Library of Congress Control Number: 2024942287

To learn more about the other great books from Fox Chapel Publishing, or to find a retailer near you, call toll-free 800-457-9112, send mail to
903 Square Street,
Mount Joy, PA 17552,
or visit us at www.FoxChapelPublishing.com.

We are always looking for talented authors. To submit an idea, please send a brief inquiry to acquisitions@foxchapelpublishing.com.

Printed in China
First printing

This book has been published with the intent to provide accurate and authoritative information in regard to the subject matter within. While every precaution has been taken in the preparation of this book, the author and publisher expressly disclaim any responsibility for any errors, omissions, or adverse effects arising from the use or application of the information contained herein.

Contents

Introduction

Whether you are new to knitting or have been knitting for decades like me, there is always a technique, stitch, or number that you need to look up for reference. This is a handy guide for all those little things you need to remember when you're knitting!

We'll first look at all the basic materials you'll need to get started on a knitting project. I'll show you step-by-step how to do basic knitting stitches and share easy stitch patterns that are great to have on the go. My design career started with shawls, so I couldn't resist sharing some of my favorite shawl tips with you. There's even more to explore—learn how to make a baby blanket to apply your skills. This pocket guide is full of information for you to enjoy. Let's get knitting!

—Jen *(she/her)*

Knitting Needles

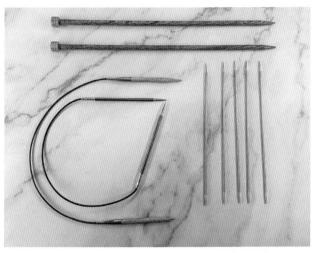

Knitting needles are available in various sizes and styles and are made from a few materials.

With so many different types of knitting needles on the market, how do you know which one is right for you? Like many things in this craft, it often comes down to personal preference as well as the project you're working on. There are lots of things to consider—some needles have pointy tips, some are blunt; there are different lengths; choosing between material types. If you can, experiment with different knitting needles to find the ones that are best for you and your individual needs.

Aluminum needles—These needles are readily available at just about every yarn and craft store, with most of them being quite affordable. Aluminum knitting needles are both lightweight and durable, and allow the stitches to slide easily, making them a great choice for most knitting projects.

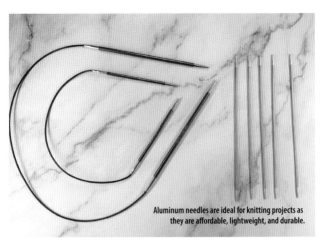

Aluminum needles are ideal for knitting projects as they are affordable, lightweight, and durable.

Wooden needles—You'll find wooden needles made from different types of wood. Because there is a little bit of "grip" to these needles, you may find that these needles are a good choice for "slick" yarn, like bamboo or silk.

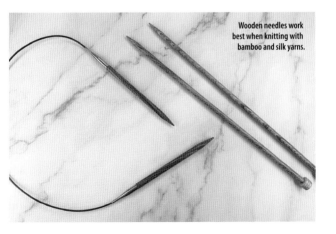

Wooden needles work best when knitting with bamboo and silk yarns.

Straight needles—When we think about knitting, we often think of straight knitting needles. They are traditional knitting needles, which come with a single point on each needle and some kind of stopper on the opposite end to prevent the stitches from sliding off. They come in a range of lengths, so you can choose the right size for your project.

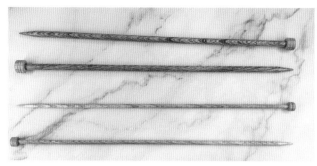

Straight needles have a stopper at one end, so the stitch does not slide off.

Circular needles—Circular needles are traditionally used to knit in the round, for projects like hats and cowls. However, you can use them for just about any knitting project. You'll also use these needles when knitting

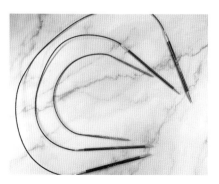

Circular needles can be used for knitting in the round as well as working back and forth in rows.

back and forth in rows—projects like shawls and blankets are often knit using circular needles to accommodate the large number of stitches on the needle. The cord also bears some of the weight of the knitted fabric, which helps your hands and wrists when knitting. Both the needles and cords come in different lengths.

Double-pointed needles (dpns)—Double-pointed needles, often abbreviated as dpns, have two points, one on each end of the needle. These needles allow you to knit in the round and are especially useful for small-circumference circular knitting, like for socks and baby items. Just like all the other needles, they come in a variety of lengths.

Double-pointed needles are great for circular knitting, such as socks.

Knitting Needle Guide

Here's a quick reference for the most common knitting needle sizes.

US Size	Millimeters	US Size	Millimeters
0	2mm	9	5.5mm
1	2.25mm	10	6mm
1.5	2.5mm	10.5	6.5mm
2	2.75mm	11	8mm
2.5	3mm	13	9mm
3	3.25mm	15	10mm
4	3.5mm	17	12mm
5	3.75mm	19	15mm
6	4mm	35	19mm
7	4.5mm	50	25mm
8	5mm	70	35mm

Yarns

~~~~~~

Besides the knitting needles, the other thing you absolutely need for your knitting project is the yarn. Choosing the yarn for your project may seem like a daunting task when there are endless possibilities for the yarn you can use. Yarn choice affects every aspect of the project, so it's important to take some time to think and plan for the yarn you're using in your project.

One of the critical factors in your yarn choice for your knitting project is the thickness of the yarn. Yarn thickness is defined by the yarn weight, and there are industry standards that almost every yarn company uses. If you find a pattern that calls for a #4/Worsted/Medium yarn, that is the yarn weight you'll want to use for your project. Changing the weight of the yarn you're using for a pattern greatly affects the gauge (page 13) of the project.

Yarn is available in a variety of textures and in every color you can imagine.

Some knitters may be comfortable with changing the weight of the yarn for a specific pattern, which is amazing; just know that most of the time, this change comes with some calculating you will have to do on your own.

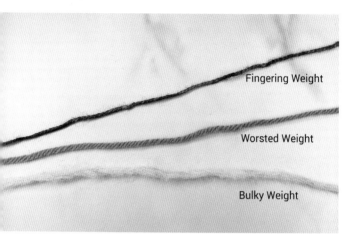

Fingering Weight

Worsted Weight

Bulky Weight

YARNS USED

For the examples in this book, I used the following yarns:

* Herrschners Worsted Yarn: *herrschners.com*
  * Used for example yarn photos.

* KnitPicks Wool of the Andes Worsted Weight: *knitpicks.com*
  * Used for Garter Stitch (page 52), Stockinette Stitch (page 54), Seed Stitch (page 53), Moss Stitch (page 55), and Basic Shawl Recipe (page 56)

* KnitPicks Swish Worsted: *knitpicks.com*
  * Used for Seaside Baby Blanket Pattern (page 61)

Yarn Weight Guide

Here's a quick reference of the Standard Yarn Weight System from the Craft Yarn Council. Remember, this chart is just a guide—it's a starting point. If you're working from a specific pattern, follow the yarn weight and gauge information for that project.

Yarn Weight & Name	Type of Yarn	Gauge in Stockinette Stitch over 4" (10.2cm)	Recommended US Needle Size
LACE 0	Lace, 10-count crochet thread	33–40 sts*	000–1*
SUPER FINE 1	Sock, Fingering, Baby	27–32 sts	1–3
FINE 2	Sport, Baby	23–26 sts	3–5
LIGHT 3	DK, Light Worsted	21–24 sts	5–7
MEDIUM 4	Worsted, Afghan, Aran	16–20 sts	7–9
BULKY 5	Bulky, Chunky	12–15 sts	9–11
SUPER BULKY 6	Super Bulky, Roving	7–11 sts	11–17
JUMBO 7	Jumbo, Roving	6 sts or less	17 and larger

* Lace yarns are typically knit using larger needles to create loose, lacy patterns.
Be sure to follow the recommendations for needle size and gauge included in your pattern.

Notions

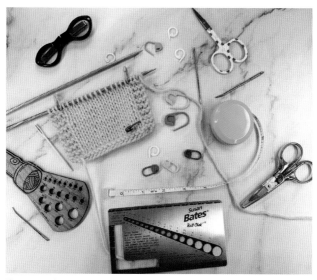

There are a number of tools you can use to make the knitting process easier.

What are notions? They are all the little tools that you need to complete your project. This can include items like stitch markers, scissors, tapestry needles, and so much more. As you continue your knitting journey, you'll find yourself adding more notions to your toolbox as needed.

Stitch markers—Stitch markers are used in projects for a variety of reasons. You may need to mark a specific stitch, or simply mark the right side or wrong side of your project. In many knitting patterns, you'll often need to section off the stitches on the knitting needle with stitch markers, whether it's to work a specific stitch pattern in between the stitch markers or to work shaping near the markers on the needle.

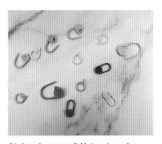

Stitch markers are available in various colors to help the marker stand out against your knitted piece.

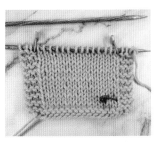

Use stitch markers to keep track of specific stitches or mark the right side or wrong side of a piece.

Scissors—When your knitting project is complete, you'll need to cut the yarn with scissors to leave a yarn tail to weave in on your piece. There are so many different types of scissors and cutting tools you can use. I personally love little folding travel scissors. They are lightweight and small enough that you can easily toss them into your project bag.

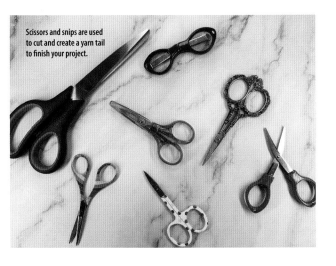

Scissors and snips are used to cut and create a yarn tail to finish your project.

Tapestry needles—Tapestry needles (also known as yarn needles or darning needles) are a necessary notion for completing your project. While these needles are often simply used to weave in the ends on a project, you can also use them for things like adding embroidery to a piece.

When choosing a tapestry needle, make sure the eye of the needle isn't too big. You want to make sure the needle can work in and out of your stitches smoothly, you don't want the eye to be so large that it starts to stretch your stitches. Many tapestry needles are sold in packs, and often one pack will contain a variety of needles.

Tapestry needles have a blunt tip and often have a bend to make it easier to insert into your project.

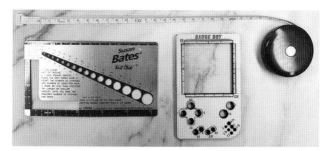

Tape measures and gauge rulers are helpful for checking the gauge size before you start a piece.

Measuring tools—Many different measuring tools serve many different purposes in knitting. You can use a tape measure for checking gauge and measurements of your project as you go. Gauge rulers are also great for checking gauge, and often come with holes for checking knitting needle and crochet hook sizes. Like everything that comes along with this hobby, you can purchase measuring tools at a big box store or find special handmade measuring notions at local yarn shops and yarn festivals.

Knitting Basics

With our tools ready, let's start on knitting basics. This includes abbreviations that you might have trouble remembering from project to project, instructions on how to check gauge, and important stitches and techniques that you'll likely be using over and over again.

Gauge

Gauge is such an important part of a knitting project. This measurement is simply the number of stitches and rows (or rounds) in a specified area (length and width). This is often written over 2" (5.1cm) or 4" (10.2cm). To measure, you'll take a tape measure and count your stitches for the area.

There are 17.5 stitches in the 4" (10.2cm) section of this row.

The gauge is measured—now what do we do with this information? You'll need to compare your gauge to the gauge listed in the pattern. If you have too many stitches, go up a needle size or two; too few stitches, use smaller-sized needles to make the stitches a little bit smaller. Remember: Every knitter tensions their yarn in different ways. The needle size on the yarn's label or in a pattern are simply a jumping off point.

Another important point about gauge is that it will affect the amount of yarn you need to complete a project. This becomes tricky on projects like blankets and scarves (or other projects that don't need to fit a body). I know most of us feel the urge to skip the gauge swatch step because we think the size of the finished object isn't super important. While that may be true, a gauge that is wildly off from the pattern can have great effects on the amount of yarn used. No one wants to run out of gradient yarn two-thirds of the way through their blanket project!

Abbreviations

Knitting patterns typically use abbreviations in the instructions. While it might seem a little confusing at first, it makes the pattern much easier to read and understand while shortening the pattern significantly. Here are some of the most common abbreviations, which are used throughout this book.

beg	begin(s), beginning
BO	bind off
cdd	central double decrease: slip first and second stitches together as if to knit, knit 1 stitch, pass two slipped stitches over the knit stitch
CO	cast on
dec	decreasing
dpn(s)	double-pointed needle(s)
foll	follows
inc	increase
k	knit
k2tog	knit two stitches together
kfb	knit into the front and back of the same stitch
kwise	knitwise

m1	with the left-hand needle, make one by lifting the strand in between the stitch just worked and the next stitch, bringing the needle from the front to back and knitting it, knitting through the back loop	**psso**	pass the slipped stitch over
		pwise	purlwise
		rem	remaining
		rep	repeat
		RS	right side
		sk2p	slip 1 stitch knitwise, k2tog, pass slipped stitch over k2tog
m1L	with the left-hand needle, make one left by lifting the strand in between the stitch just worked and the next stitch, bringing the needle from the front to back and knitting it, knitting through the back loop	**sl**	slip stitch purlwise
		sm	slip marker
		ssk	slip a stitch as if to knit to the right needle, slip a second stitch as if to knit to the right needle, slip both stitches back to the left needle and knit together through the back loops
m1R	with the left-hand needle, make one right by lifting the strand in between the stitch just worked and the next stitch, bringing the needle from the back to front and knitting it	**St st**	stockinette stitch
		st(s)	stitch(es)
		tbl	through the back loop
		tog	together
		WS	wrong side
p	purl	**wyib**	with yarn in back
patt	pattern	**wyif**	with yarn in front
pm	place marker	**yo**	yarn over

Slip Knot

A slip knot is the first step for starting most knitting projects. There are lots of ways to make a slip knot. This is the method I like to use when teaching others about knitting basics. It's both easy to do and easy to learn!

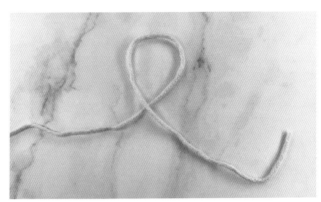

1. Leaving a yarn tail of approximately 4"–6" (10.2–15.2cm), create a loop with the yarn tail going over the working yarn (the yarn coming from the ball of yarn).

2. Take the loop and fold down over the working yarn. You have something that looks a little like a pretzel.

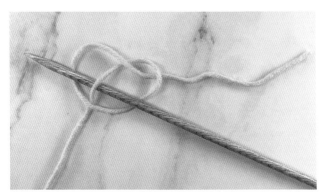

3. You'll see three strands, with the center strand being the working yarn. With the knitting needle, go over the bottom strand, under the middle strand, and over the top strand.

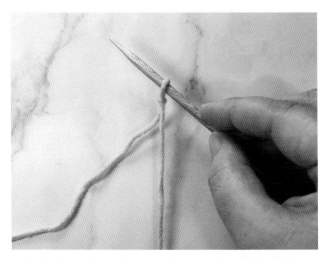

4. Pull on both yarn tail and working yarn to tighten loop on the needle. Your slip knot is complete.

Casting On

Casting on is the first step in starting your knitting project. There's no shortage of ways to cast on. Here are a few of the most common ones you'll use in your projects.

Knitted Cast On

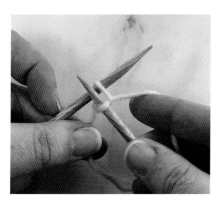

1. Leaving a yarn tail of approximately 4"–6" (10.2–15.2cm), start with a slip knot on the left-hand needle. Insert the right-hand needle into the slip knot as if to knit, yarn over, and pull a loop through.

2. Transfer the new stitch from the right-hand needle to the left-hand needle.

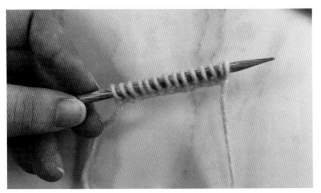

3. Knit into the last stitch on the left-hand needle, and transfer the new stitch back to the left-hand needle until you have the correct number of stitches.

Long Tail Cast On

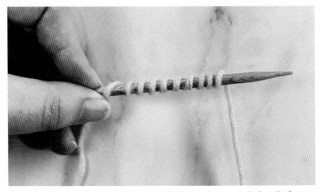

1. Leaving a yarn tail of approximately 4"–6" (10.2–15.2cm), estimate the length of yarn tail needed by wrapping the yarn around the needle 10 times. This is approximately the yarn needed for 10 stitches in the long tail cast on. Unravel off needle and use that length.

2. With the knitting needle in your right hand, hold the yarn in your left hand so that the long tail is going over your thumb and the working yarn (the yarn going to your ball of yarn) is around your index finger.

3. Maneuver the needle under the loop of yarn on your thumb.

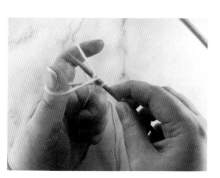

4. Bring the needle over to the yarn on your index finger and "catch" the yarn on the needle.

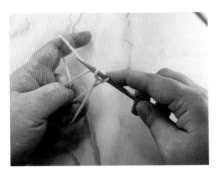

5. Draw the yarn through the loop on your thumb.

6. Drop the yarn from your thumb and tighten the stitch (don't overtighten) to the needle.

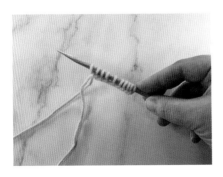

7. Repeat these steps until you have the desired number of stitches cast onto the needle.

Garter Tab Cast On for Top-Down Shawls

I've written a bunch of books about shawl knitting, so I must share this cast on for top-down shawls. This cast on is typically worked as follows. Refer to the pattern you're knitting for the specific number of stitches to cast on and how many rows are to be worked; we're looking at the classic example here that ends with nine stitches on the needle.

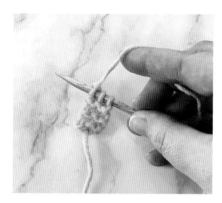

1. Using the long tail cast on (page 23) or cast on of choice, cast on three stitches and knit six rows.

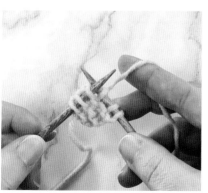

2. Rotate the work 90 degrees clockwise, and pick up three stitches evenly along the left edge. Try to insert the needle into each of the three bumps on the edge of the tab.

3. Knit the three stitches from step 2—six stitches on the needle.

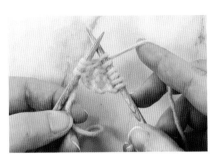

4. Rotate the work 90 degrees clockwise again, and pick up three stitches evenly from the cast-on edge.

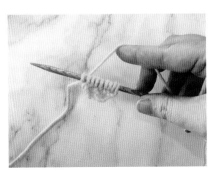

5. Knit the three stitches from step 4—nine stitches on the needle. Turn your work and continue with the pattern as written.

The Knit Stitch

1. With yarn in back (behind the work), insert the right needle into the front of the first stitch on the left needle, from left to right.

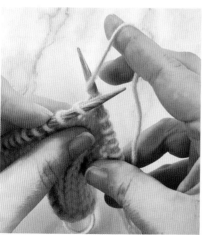

2. Wrap the yarn counterclockwise around the right needle.

3. Bring the yarn through the stitch on the left needle.

4. Remove the stitch from the left needle. The new stitch is on the right needle.

The Purl Stitch

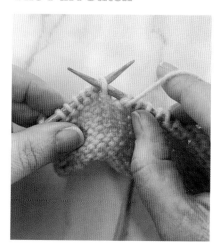

1. With the yarn in front, insert the right needle into the front leg of the first stitch on the left needle, from right to left.

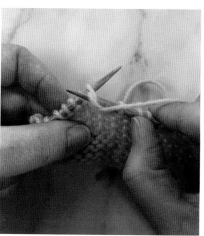

2. Wrap the yarn counterclockwise around the right needle.

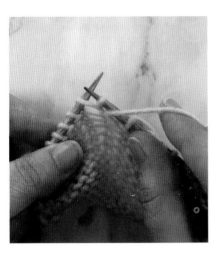

3. With the yarn on the needle, bring the right needle back through the stitch from left to right.

4. Remove the stitch from the left needle. The new stitch is on the right needle.

Increasing

There will be instances in knitting patterns where you'll need to increase the number of stitches on the needle or create other details and shaping with increases. There are whole books dedicated to increasing and decreasing in knitting—I'm sharing the most common ones here.

Yarn Over

1. When working in knit stitches, bring the yarn from the back of the work in between the needles to the front of the work.

2. Bring the yarn up and over the right needle to the back of the work.

3. Work the next stitch as written in your pattern. The yarn over stitch has been created.

Make One

The make one stitch is just that—you're making a stitch where there wasn't one before.

Make One Left

This stitch is the traditional make 1 (m1) stitch. If there are directional increases in a pattern, you may also see this abbreviated as m1L (make 1 left).

1. With the left-hand needle and yarn in back, lift the strand in between the stitch just worked and the next stitch, bringing the needle from the front to back.

2. Insert the right-hand needle from the front to back through the back of the stitch.

3. Wrap the yarn to create a knit stitch, dropping the strand off the left-hand needle to complete the stitch.

Make One Right

1. With the left-hand needle and yarn in back, lift the strand in between the stitch just worked and the next stitch, bringing the needle from the back to front.

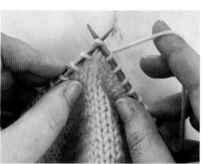

2. Insert the right-hand needle from the front to back through the front of the stitch.

3. Wrap the yarn to create a knit stitch, dropping the strand off the left-hand needle to complete the stitch.

Knit Front and Back

1. With the yarn in back, knit the next stitch on the left-hand needle, leaving the stitch on the needle.

2. Insert the right-hand needle into the back of the stitch on the left-hand needle.

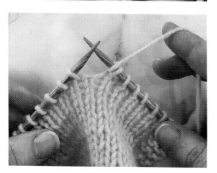

3. Knit the stitch, dropping the stitch from the left-hand needle, completing the stitch.

Decreasing

Like increasing, there's no shortage of ways to decrease the number of stitches on the needles. Here are some of the most common ones.

Knit Two Together

1. With the yarn in back, insert the right-hand needle into the second stitch, then the first stitch on the left-hand needle, from left to right.

2. Wrap the yarn around the right-hand needle to create a knit stitch, dropping the two stitches off the left-hand needle to complete the stitch.

Slip Slip Knit

1. With the yarn in back, slip a stitch as if to knit from the left-hand needle to the right-hand needle.

2. Slip a second stitch as if to knit from the left-hand needle to the right-hand needle.

3. Slip both stitches back to the left-hand needle and knit together through the back loops.

Slip One, Knit Two Together, Pass the Slipped Stitch Over

1. With the yarn in back, slip a stitch as if to knit from the left-hand needle to the right-hand needle.

2. Knit the next two stitches together (k2tog).

3. Pass the slipped stitch over the k2tog.

Central Double Decrease

1. With the yarn in back, slip as if to knit together the first and second stitches on the left-hand needle to the right-hand needle.

2. Knit the next stitch.

3. Pass the two slipped stitches together over the knit stitch.

Binding Off

Once your project is complete, you'll need to finish it by binding off the remaining stitches. Like many things in knitting, there's no shortage of ways to complete this task.

Knitwise Bind Off

1. Knit the first two stitches independently—two stitches on the right-hand needle.

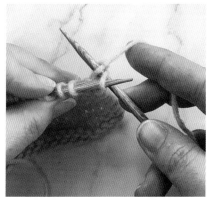

2. From the front, insert the left-hand needle into the first stitch that was knit.

3. Pass the first stitch over the second stitch and off the needle—one stitch on the right-hand needle.

4. Knit the next stitch— two stitches on the right-hand needle.

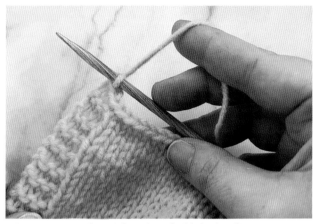

5. Repeat steps 2–4 until one stitch remains on the right-hand needle.

6. Trim the yarn, leaving an approximately 4"–6" (10.2–15.2cm) tail to weave in later. Draw the yarn through the last loop to fasten off.

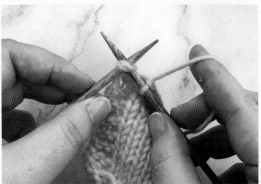

If your last bind-off stitch looks a little loose, try working the bind off to the last two stitches and then knitting the last two stitches together. Complete the final bind-off step as usual.

Purlwise Bind Off

1. Purl the first two stitches independently— two stitches on the right-hand needle.

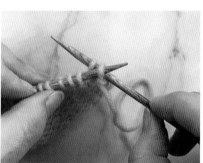

2. From the front, insert the left-hand needle into the first stitch that was purled.

3. Pass the first stitch over the second stitch and off the needle—one stitch on the right-hand needle.

4. Purl the next stitch—two stitches on the right-hand needle.

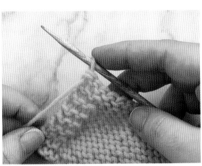

5. Repeat steps 2–4 until one stitch remains on the right-hand needle.

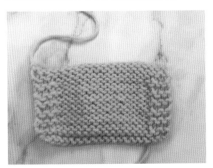

6. Trim the yarn, leaving an approximately 4"–6" (10.2–15.2cm) tail to weave in later. Draw the yarn through the last loop to fasten off.

Shawl Bind Off

The following is my favorite bind off for when knitting shawls or other projects where I need a stretchy, loose bind-off edge. If you tend to bind off tightly, try using a needle one or two sizes larger as well.

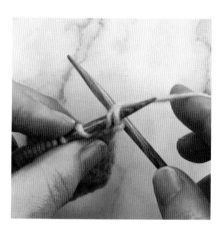

1. Knit the first two stitches together through the back loop.

2. Slip the stitch purlwise from the right needle to the left needle.

3. Knit two together through the back loops.

4. Repeat steps 2 and 3 until one stitch remains on the right-hand needle.

5. Trim the yarn, leaving an approximately 4"–6" (10.2–15.2cm) tail to weave in later. Draw the yarn through the last loop to fasten off.

Finishing: Fasten Off & Weave in Ends

Finishing your project can involve a lot of different techniques. Most commonly, you'll need to fasten off the project and weave in all the ends.

To fasten off, simply trim the working yarn (the yarn going to your ball of yarn) with scissors, leaving a tail about 6"–8" (15.2–20.3cm) long. Bring the tail of the yarn through the final working loop.

With the project fastened off, it's time to weave in any remaining yarn tails. If there is an obvious wrong side to the piece, weave in the ends on the wrong side of the fabric. Use a tapestry needle to work the tail in and out of the stitches. Use a tapestry needle with an appropriately-sized eye, and take care not to pull on this tail too much while weaving in the end—you don't want to distort the fabric! With a light hand, weave in the end. Trim the remaining yarn tail.

Slipping Stitches

Slipping one or more stitches is a common technique you'll see in many knitting projects. There are different ways the stitch can be slipped—here are basic slipped-stitch techniques you'll find.

With Yarn in Front

Keep the yarn to the front of your work, instead of behind.

If a pattern says to slip stitch with yarn in front, keep the yarn to the front of the work as you slip the stitch. Unless otherwise indicated in the pattern, the right side/wrong side of the fabric doesn't matter here—with yarn in front means in front of the work as you are currently looking at it.

With Yarn in Back

Keep the yarn to behind your work, instead of in front.

If a pattern says to slip stitch with yarn in back, keep the yarn to the back of the work as you slip the stitch. Unless otherwise indicated in the pattern, the right side/wrong side of the fabric doesn't matter here—with yarn in back means in back of the work as you are currently looking at it.

Slip Stitch Purlwise

If a pattern tells you to slip a stitch and does not indicate knitwise or purlwise, in general, the stitch is assumed to be slipped purlwise.

1. Insert the right-hand needle into the stitch on the left-hand needle as if you are going to purl the stitch.

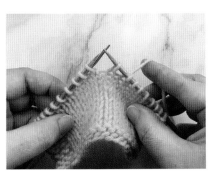

2. Do *not* purl the stitch. Instead, slide it off the left-hand needle to the right-hand needle.

Slip Stitch Knitwise

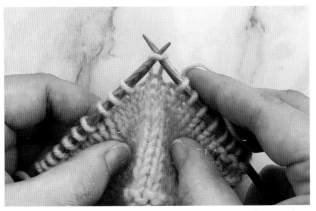

1. Insert the right-hand needle into the stitch on the left-hand needle as if you are going to knit the stitch.

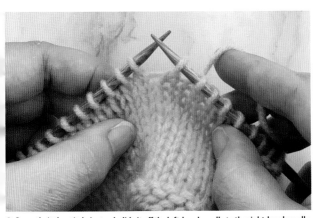

2. Do *not* knit the stitch. Instead, slide it off the left-hand needle to the right-hand needle.

Stitch Patterns

The following are a few of the most beloved stitch patterns for knitting. You can use these alone or in combination to create unique pieces.

Garter Stitch

Cast on the desired number of stitches and work as follows:

All Rows: Knit all stitches.

Garter stitches are made by knitting every row.

Seed Stitch

Worked over an odd number of stitches as follows:

All Rows: (k1, p1) to the last stitch, k1.

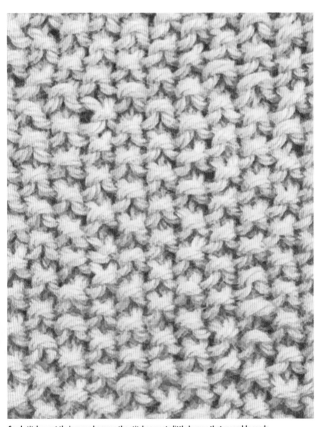

Seed stitches get their name because the stitches create little bumps that resemble seeds.

Stockinette Stitch

Cast on the desired number of stitches and work as follows:

Row 1 (RS): Knit all stitches.

Row 2 (WS): Purl all stitches.

Rep Rows 1 and 2 for pattern.

Stockinette stitches are created by alternating rows of knit and purl stitches.

TIP:

Remember, stockinette stitch naturally curls on itself. In many cases, you'll want to consider adding some kind of border (garter stitch, moss stitch, etc.) to the edges for the fabric to lay flat.

Moss Stitch

This stitch is sometimes referred to as the American Moss Stitch or Irish Moss Stitch.

Worked over an even number of stitches as follows:

Row 1 (RS): *k1, p1; rep from * to end.

Row 2 (WS): rep Row 1.

Row 3: *p1, k1; rep from * to end.

Row 4: rep Row 3.

Rep Rows 1–4 for pattern.

Moss stitches are created by knitting two rows of the same sequence of knit and purl stitches before alternating the stitches.

Basic Shawl Recipe

You can use knitting projects, such as this top-down triangle shawl, to try out the stitch patterns presented in this book.

Here's a pattern recipe that perhaps you didn't know you needed—the top-down triangle shawl! This classic shawl shape will never go out of style, and it's a great project to practice basic shaping. This pattern recipe is worked primarily in the stockinette stitch; however, you can use this as a blank canvas for other stitch patterns. Don't be afraid to play around with this shawl shape and make it your own.

SUGGESTED YARN AMOUNTS

- Sock/Fingering Weight—400 yds (365m) for shawlette; 600 yds (550m) for shawl
- Sport/DK Weight—350 yds (320m) for shawlette; 525 yds (480m) for shawl
- Worsted Weight—300 yds (275m) for shawlette; 450 yds (410m) for shawl

SUGGESTED NEEDLE SIZES

- Fingering/Sock Weight—US 5–US 6 (3.75–4mm) circular needle, 24" (61cm) cable or longer
- Sport/DK Weight—US 6–US 7 (4–4.5mm) circular needle, 24" (61cm) cable or longer
- Worsted Weight—US 7–US 8 (4.5–5mm) circular needle, 24" (61cm) cable or longer

SUGGESTED APPROXIMATE GAUGES

- Fingering/Sock Weight—20 sts and 26 rows = 4" (10.2cm) in St st, blocked
- Sport/DK Weight—18 sts and 24 rows = 4" (10.2cm) in St st, blocked
- Worsted Weight—16 sts and 22 rows = 4" (10.2cm) in St st, blocked

OTHER SUPPLIES NEEDED

- 4 stitch markers
- Tapestry needle
- Blocking supplies (see Finishing)

Pattern Notes

If you plan to make a really large shawl, you may want to use a longer circular needle to accommodate the large number of stitches that will be on the needles.

Gauge is not critical for this pattern; however, a different gauge will affect the size of shawl and amount of yarn used.

This pattern is a basic, recipe-style pattern. The beauty of this pattern is you can knit your shawl as big as you like. There are suggested yarn amounts and gauges listed to help you get started.

If you do not want to use the garter tab cast on, just cast on 9 sts and continue the pattern as written. This will slightly affect the look of the shawl at the top-center; however, this is a minor detail—do what makes you happy when knitting your shawl.

MAKE IT YOUR OWN!

Don't want to purl? Don't want to worry about curl? Simply work your shawl entirely in garter stitch: knit all stitches on wrong side rows.

Instructions

Work the garter tab CO (page 22) as follows:
CO 3 sts. Knit 6 rows. Turn work 90 degrees clockwise, and pick up and knit 3 sts along the left edge. Turn work 90 degrees clockwise, and pick up and knit 3 sts from CO edge—9 sts.

Next Row (WS): k3, p3, k3.

Row 1 (RS): k3, pm, yo, k1, yo, pm, k1 (this is the center st), pm, yo, k1, yo, pm, k3—4 sts inc; 13 sts.

Row 2 (WS): k3, purl to the last 3 sts, k3.

Row 3: k3, sm, yo, knit to next marker, yo, sm, k1, sm, yo, knit to last marker, yo, sm, k3—4 sts inc; 17 sts.

Rep Rows 2 and 3 to desired size, ending with Row 3.

Final Row (WS): Knit all sts, removing stitch markers along the way.

Finishing

BO all sts loosely using the Shawl Bind Off (page 46) or your desired stretchy bind off.

Wet block the shawl, if desired, as follows:

Soak the shawl in warm water, adding a wool wash if you like. After soaking 30–60 minutes, remove and ring it out with a towel. Use either blocking wires or pins to block it to the specified size. For a triangular shawl, I like to run a wire along the top edge, and then carefully stretch it out and pin the wires in place on a blocking board to dry. For the side edges, run a wire through the points you want to pull out, and then carefully stretch out the lace and pin the wires in place.

TIP:

Because this shawl is worked primarily in stockinette stitch (page 54), the bottom edge may curl, even when working the final WS row as knit stitches. To avoid this, you can work all knit stitches on WS rows for the final few rows of your shawl. It's a nice little garter stitch detail, and it helps the edge from curling!

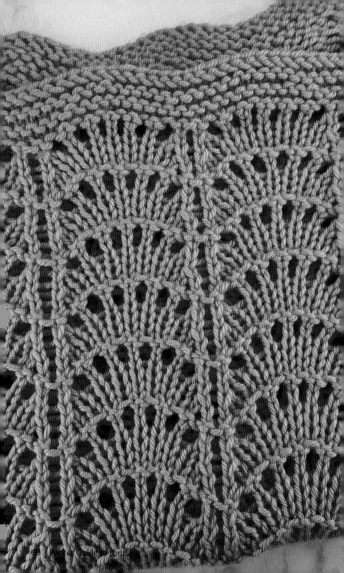

Seaside Baby Blanket Pattern

Lovely lace waves adorn this baby blanket. Strategically placed increases and decreases create an allover, undulating stitch pattern that's a delight to knit.

Finished Size: 32" x 44" (81.3 x 111.8cm)

Gauge

16 sts and 14 rows = 4" (10.2cm) in pattern, blocked

Pattern Notes

Gauge is not critical for this pattern; however, a different gauge will affect the amount of yarn needed as well as the finished size of the blanket.

In the Main Blanket Pattern, the stitch count changes with the completion of every right side row. On Rows 1 and 3, the stitch count is decreased. On Row 5, the stitch count returns to its original 129 stitches once the row is complete.

The two stitch markers in the pattern are to mark the border stitches on each edge of the blanket. Some knitters like to mark each stitch repeat with markers to keep track of their place and to be able to identify mistakes more easily. You'll need 10 additional stitch markers should you decide to mark each stitch repeat in the pattern.

TOOLS AND MATERIALS

- 660 yds (600m) of worsted weight (Medium #4) yarn
  - I used 6 skeins of KnitPicks Swish Worsted, 100% superwash merino wool, 110 yds (100m)/1.75oz (50g), in the color Conch
- US 8 (5mm) circular needle, 32" (81.3cm) cable or longer
- 2 stitch markers
- Tapestry needle

Continue to hone your knitting skills and practice stitches, such as the garter stitch, by crafting this baby blanket.

Instructions

CO 129 sts (or any multiple of 13 plus 12 sts).
Set-Up Row (WS): sl1 wyif, k4, pm, knit to last 5 sts, pm, k5.

Beginning Garter Stitch Border

Rows 1 (RS)–6 (WS): sl1 wyif, k4, sm, knit to marker, sm, k5.

Main Blanket Pattern

Using the chart or written instructions below, work Rows 1–6 until the blanket measures 42" (106.7cm) from cast-on edge or 1" (2.5cm) less than desired length, ending with Row 6.

Row 1 (RS): sl1 wyif, k4, sm, k1, *ssk, k9, k2tog; rep from * to 1 st before marker, k1, sm, k5—111 sts.

Row 2 (WS): sl1 wyif, k4, sm, purl to marker, sm, k5.

Row 3: sl1 wyif, k4, sm, *ssk, k7, k2tog; rep from * to 1 st before marker, k1, sm, k5—93 sts.

Row 4: sl1 wyif, k4, sm, purl to marker, sm, k5.

Row 5: sl1 wyif, k4, sm, *ssk, (yo, k1) 5 times, yo, k2tog; rep from * to 1 st before marker, k1, sm, k5—129 sts.

Row 6: sl1 wyif, k4, sm, knit to marker, sm, k5.

Rep Rows 1–6 for patt.

Ending Garter Stitch Border

Rows 1 (RS)–6 (WS): sl1 wyif, k4, sm, knit to marker, sm, k5.

Finishing

BO all sts loosely on RS. Weave in ends. Lightly steam block if desired.

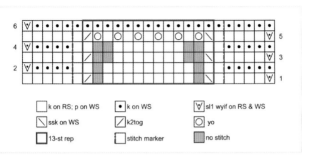

Main Blanket Pattern Chart

BLANKET SIZE GUIDE		
	Length	**Width**
Car Seat	48" (121.9cm)	36" (91.4cm)
Receiving	40" (101.6cm)	40" (101.6cm)
Crib	60" (152.4cm)	45" (114.3cm)
Toddler	48" (121.9cm)	42" (106.7cm)
Throw	72" (182.9cm)	60" (152.4cm)
Twin	96" (243.8cm)	66" (167.6cm)
Full/Queen	100" (254cm)	90" (228.6cm)
King	110" (279.4cm)	110" (279.4cm)

About the Author

Jen Lucas has been knitting for over two decades. She has designed hundreds of knitting and crochet patterns for yarn companies, magazines, and books, in addition to her dozens of self-published designs. Jen is the author of several knitting books, including the best seller, *Sock-Yarn Shawls*. She lives in Northern Illinois with her husband, Alex, and a home full of crafts. Learn more about Jen at *craftyjencrafts.com*.